Ground-beetle (*Caloso* *...alidum*), natural size.

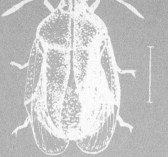

*Eurygaster alternatus;* wings partly open. (Line shows natural size.)

A Species of *Phrynus*, about life-size.

*b*

*a*

Spiderwort Owlet-moth (*Prodenia flavimedia*). *a*, larva; *b*, wings of moth.

The ...
ste...
*a*, ...
tin...
ve...
the...

*Ephemeridæ.*
...uropean May-fly (*Eph-rulgata*) and its sub-
...arva.

Thighed Metapodius (*Metapo-dius femoratus*).

Bombardier-beetle (*Bra-chinus stygicornis*). (Verti-cal line shows natural size.)

The Cucujo.

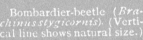

*Podisus placidus.*
*a*, enlarged; *b*, natural size.

H...
Tail...
ing ho...
dal ve...
dal r...
bones;...
esses;...
united...
for the...
ral spi...

*Libellulidæ.*
Development of a dragon-fly, showing the subaquatic larva, ...emergence from the pupa, and ...he adult fully winged insect.

A Flea (*Pulex irri-tans*).
*a*, puncturing stylets of the proboscis.

A Bristletail (*Lepisma sac-charina*). $^{5}/_{1}$

*Phymata erosa.*

*Atypus sulzeri.* (Vertical line shows natural size.)

Grape-vine    Fidia (*F. viticida*). (Line sh...ws natural size.)

Bacon-beet'e.

One o...

A...

dragonfly

dragon

# fly

by

Ting Morris

illustrated by

Desiderio Sanzi

designed by

Deb Miner

A⁺

SMART APPLE MEDIA

During the summer months, **you may see them darting past you near lakes and ponds**. Watch as they skim over the water. Their eyes are sparkling beads, their bodies are brilliant jewels, and their wings are like shimmering gauze.

Who are these acrobats of the air? **Turn the page and take a closer look.**

**They are
called dragonflies,
and they are some of
the most beautiful of all insects.**

Dragonflies are also among the fastest-flying and oldest insects in the world.

Look how this blue dragonfly's wings flash in the sun. He can use one on its own or two at a time in opposite directions, so he can hover in the air and keep watch over his pond. Sometimes he even flies backward, but now he's using all four wings to zoom across the water at top speed. What has he spotted?

## LONG, LONG AGO

Dragonflies existed 300 million years ago, before the age of the dinosaurs. Fossils show that these prehistoric insects were much larger than today's dragonflies, with a wingspan of more than 24 inches (60 cm). They were no easy catch for a hungry pterodactyl!

## A DRAGONFLY'S BODY

A dragonfly's body has three parts—the HEAD, the trunk (called the THORAX), and the long, thin ABDOMEN, or stomach.

Two enormous COMPOUND EYES cover most of the head, which can swivel in any direction. There are also three simple eyes on top of the head and two small feelers (called ANTENNAE). The MOUTH has jaws that work like saws. Dragonflies eat insects.

Six long, bristly LEGS and four large WINGS are attached to the thorax. A network of VEINS stiffens the see-through wings. Although the dragonfly's legs are almost useless for walking, they are good for perching, as well as catching and holding food.

The tail-like abdomen has 10 segments that look like rings stuck together. Males have big CLASPERS at the end of the abdomen; females have delicate little CLAWS.

Dragonflies breathe through tiny holes in their bodies called SPIRACLES.

## SKY RACERS

Dragonflies can fly at speeds of up to 38 miles (60 km) per hour. Some have even been clocked going more than 56 miles (90 km) per hour!

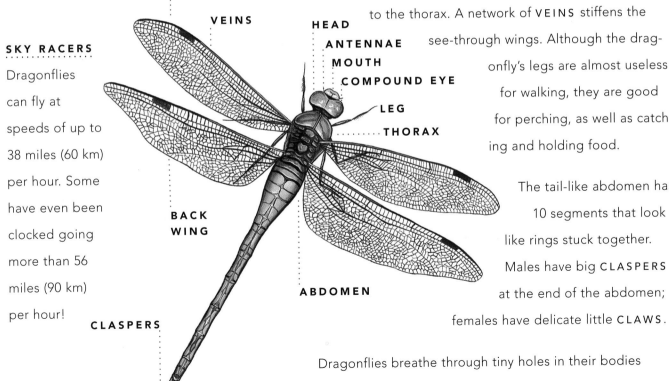

FRONT WING
VEINS
HEAD
ANTENNAE
MOUTH
COMPOUND EYE
LEG
THORAX
BACK WING
ABDOMEN
CLASPERS

7

This blue dragonfly is master of the pond, but a rival has dared to enter his hunting ground.

**ON HOME GROUND**

A male dragonfly chooses a place near a pond, river, or lake that will make a good breeding site for a female's eggs. Once he has chased away other males, female dragon-flies come and visit.

This is his chosen place for meeting a mate, and he doesn't want any other males around.

The speckled intruder is taking a risk. **The two male dragonflies battle it out in the air.** Look—they are tumbling toward the pond! Just before they hit the water, the speckled rival gives up and zooms away.

## FOOD BASKETS ● ● ● ● ● ● ● ● ●➤

Dragonflies hold their legs together to form
a basket while they fly very fast to catch
insects. After catching a victim, they grab it
with their strong jaws and eat it in flight.
They can catch insects as big as butterflies.

## BATTLING IT OUT

For a week or more,
battles are fought in
the air between males.
Usually the defender
will fly under the
attacker and push
him away from the
water surface, which
is his territory.

## SIXTY THOUSAND VIEWS

Each compound eye has
30,000 lenses. That's like
having 60,000 eyes. The
dragonfly can see everything
around it, including moving
objects up to 33 feet (10 m)
away. It's no wonder that
nothing escapes the dragonfly, especially harmful insects
such as mosquitoes.

9

The blue dragonfly allows females from all around to move into his territory. They are all welcome at his pond, no matter what kind they are. But he is waiting for a particular female.

**Today a beautiful new arrival has caught his eye.** Her body is green, and her wings and markings look like his—she is his own kind. He whizzes across the pond and chases her. Then they pair up and fly through the air together. High up in a tree, the two dragonflies mate.

**SPEED COUNTS**

Sometimes two males chase the same female. The fastest flyer wins the right to mate with her.

## MATING ●●●●●●●●●●●●●●●➤

Male and female dragonflies and damselflies sometimes mate in flight. The male holds the female by her neck with his claspers. She needs his sperm for her eggs.

➤●●●● **MATCHSTICK RELATIVES**

Damselflies are small, slim relatives of dragonflies. Most damselflies are no bigger than a matchstick and are weak flyers. But they are even more colorful than their big, speedy relatives. When damselflies rest, they hold their wings together over their body. Dragonflies rest with their wings open.

11

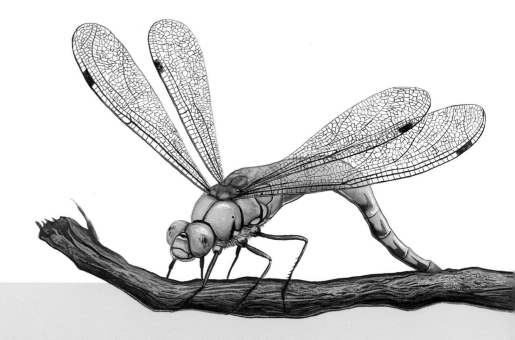

The green female flies back to the pond and hovers low over the water. She doesn't want to be disturbed while she is searching for a safe place to lay her eggs. With her body curled forward, she looks like a stinging insect. This is a clever disguise—no one will bother her now.

**She's found a floating stem and is pushing her eggs into it, one by one.** Sometimes females are guarded by their mates, but if they are as big and strong as this one, they don't need any help.

12

### CAMOUFLAGE

Female dragonflies are usually less colorful than males. Sky-blue and bright red males mate with females that are dullish green, brown, and yellow. Dull colors help when it comes time to lay eggs, since enemies have a harder time spotting the busy mothers.

### ON GUARD

The blue damselfly guards the female while she is underwater, pushing her eggs into a pond plant.

### EGGS GALORE

Female dragonflies look for a wet place to lay their eggs. Each egg is no bigger than the head of a pin.

Some eggs are long and thin or oval.

Some dragonfly mothers drop round eggs into the water. They form sticky groups on under-water plants.

13

Three weeks have passed, and the eggs are hatching. The tiny creatures inside are dragonfly nymphs. They are in a hurry to push their way out and dive into the water. **The pond is their nursery, where the nymphs will grow and change.**

Can you see their parents? They are darting through the air, but their days are numbered. They will never meet their young. A grown-up dragonfly's life lasts only one summer. But their water babies will live at the bottom of this pond for two years or more.

**EGG-BOUND**

Some eggs hatch a few weeks after being laid. Others spend the winter safe in their damp stems.

14

## QUICK CHANGE

A newly hatched nymph doesn't hang on to its skin for long. Some wait only seconds, and certainly no more than a few hours, before they split their skin. A new, larger skin has formed underneath, and when that gets tight, it will be time for another change.

## HEAD FIRST ● ● ● ● ● ●➤

The nymph pushes its way out, head first. Young nymphs have no wings. They are almost see-through, which helps them hide from their enemies in the water.

## HARD ADULTS

Like all insects, dragonflies have a hard skeleton, called an exoskeleton, on the outside of their bodies. The changes a dragonfly goes through from egg to nymph to adult are called metamorphosis.

**Life underwater is dangerous for small nymphs.** The pond is full of hungry creatures looking for a tasty meal. Hiding on the bottom helps, but every nymph must find food so it can grow strong for the many changes that lie ahead.

Like their parents, dragonfly nymphs are great hunters, and there's no shortage of water fleas to feed on. If they are under enemy attack, the nymphs can dart away in a flash.

### THE YOUNG NYMPH

The nymph has a thick body, big head, mouth, and no wings. But every time it changes, it looks more like its dragonfly parents. After the fourth change of skin, its eyes are bigger, and tiny wing cases appear on its back. Dragonfly nymphs molt, or shed their skins, up to 15 times.

**TAIL FEATHERS** ● ● ● ●▶

Damselfly nymphs have gills on their tails. The gills look like three feathers and are sometimes snapped off by fish or other attackers. The nymphs don't mind, because they can still breathe without them. The feathers seem to be simply a clever way of tricking enemies.

● **JETTING OFF**

Nymphs breathe through gills in the tip of their abdomen, so water passes in and out of their body all the time. They use this pumping action to move about. When in danger, the nymph presses the water out, which jets it away quickly.

17

MIDGE LARVA

Two summers have passed, and this
is the nymph's last winter in the water.
**It is now an expert hunter and is
feared by most small pond animals.**
Even other nymphs may be on the menu.
The nymph catches anything around with its large
bottom lip. This gruesome weapon is called a
mask and has a pair of pincers at the tip. The
nymph usually lies in wait for its prey, hidden in
the mud. Can you spot it? You'll see that it's
much darker now.
As soon as a tadpole or a small fish swims
by, the nymph shoots out its mask and grabs
the passing victim with the pincers.

CADDIS-FLY
LARVA

18

**TADPOLES**

**WATER-BEETLE
LARVA**

**WATCH OUT!**

Most nymphs hide
in the mud, keep
very still, and wait
for their food to
come to them.
Some hunt among
the weeds. Fish
and ducks are a
constant danger
to them.

● **MASKED RAIDER**

A folding lower lip,
called a mask, is hidden
under the nymph's
mouth. This mask works
like an arm. The nymph
shoots out the mask to
capture prey and then
draws its victim back to
its real jaws. The mask
is half as long as the
nymph's body.

**WHAT'S ON THE MENU?**
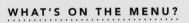
The pond is well-stocked
with food for growing
nymphs. Hungry young
dragonflies love insect grubs
and other tiny creatures.

The dragonfly nymph crawls up a stem by the light of the moon. Then it looks down on the pond, where it has lived for two years, and breaks out of its skin. **On this warm summer night, it has turned into an adult dragonfly.**

But why doesn't it fly away? Look at its wings—they are stunted and crumpled. The young dragonfly is pumping blood into its wings to make them big and strong. It will have to stay here until its body hardens. All of this must happen before the sun comes up. If a hungry bird or a hunting spider sees it now, the helpless dragonfly cannot escape.

### RIGHT TIMING

Nymphs change into dragonflies only in the summer and always on a warm day. They move into shallow waters a few days before and check out the site. Then they slip back into deeper waters and wait for the right time.

20

## THE BIG CHANGE

1. Under the cover of darkness, the dragonfly nymph comes out of the pond and climbs onto a reed or rock. It is now fully grown, up to two inches (5 cm) long, and ready for its final molt.

2. When it has dried off, the skin splits along the back. The new dragonfly pulls out its head, the front of its body, and its legs. But they are still soft and weak.

3. The dragonfly rests with its head held back until its legs are hard.

4. The dragonfly pulls the rest of its body out and hangs on to the old skin while it is drying out. It pumps blood into its wings, and after a few minutes they are much bigger.

5. Four hours later, the dragonfly's body is straight and hard. But the shiny wings are still damp. The dragonfly will have to wait another hour before it can fly away.

When the dragonfly feels that her wings are good and strong, she spreads them wide. Look how the shiny wings shimmer in the rising sun. **Now she is ready to fly.** She knows there's danger about and is in a hurry to leave the pond.

## AIR SAFETY

While they are flying, dragonflies are safe from most attackers. They are too fast to be caught. Birds such as swallows and falcons are their only enemies in the air.

## COLORING UP

The dragonfly's brilliant colors take a week to develop. During that time, they usually stay away from water. You can tell how old a dragonfly is by its brightness. When the wings and body are fully colored, the dragonfly is old enough to mate. Most dragonflies live for only two to four weeks, and damselflies live up to two weeks.

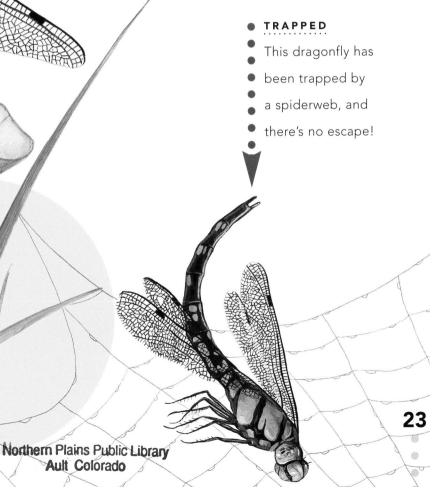

## QUICK GETAWAY

While the dragonfly is waiting for its wings to dry out, it is in great danger. Its main enemies are birds and spiders. Many helpless youngsters are eaten before they can fly. As soon as they can spread their wings, they leave the site in an almost vertical takeoff. New dragonflies often fly many miles away from the water.

## TRAPPED

This dragonfly has been trapped by a spiderweb, and there's no escape!

23

After about a week, an adult dragonfly is ready to look for a mate. The meeting place is always near water.

On the day the young dragonfly tried out her wings, many other speedy flyers took to the air. They left the pond and went hunting in the woods and fields nearby. If you see a dragonfly, don't hurt or catch it. They are helpful creatures, since they capture mosquitoes and other biting insects.

**After spending a week flying about and catching insects, our dragonfly has arrived at a beautiful lake.** She hovers over the water, watching and waiting.

She's looking at the big blue dragonfly that's darting past. This part of the lake is his territory, and he's on the lookout. Can you guess what happens next?

## MOST LIKE IT HOT

There are more than 5,000 different kinds of dragonflies. Most live in hot climates. True dragonflies have thicker bodies and bigger eyes than their damselfly relatives.

## FINAL CHANGE

Nymphs generally leave the water for their final change within a few days of each other. If there's plenty of food underwater and the nymph is a good hunter, it grows quickly. Some fully grown nymphs go through a resting stage in spring. This allows other nymphs to catch up and become adult dragonflies at the same time.

## HAWKERS AND...

There are two groups of true dragonflies, called hawkers and darters. Hawkers, like our blue dragonfly, spend a lot of time patrolling their stretch of water in search of food and a mate. They are powerful fliers and hunt high in the air, many feet from the ground.

## DARTERS

Darters have a shorter body and usually live near swamps. They choose a perch, such as a reed or twig, on which they sun themselves and watch for prey or rival males. Throughout the day, they dart from their perch, catch food, and return.

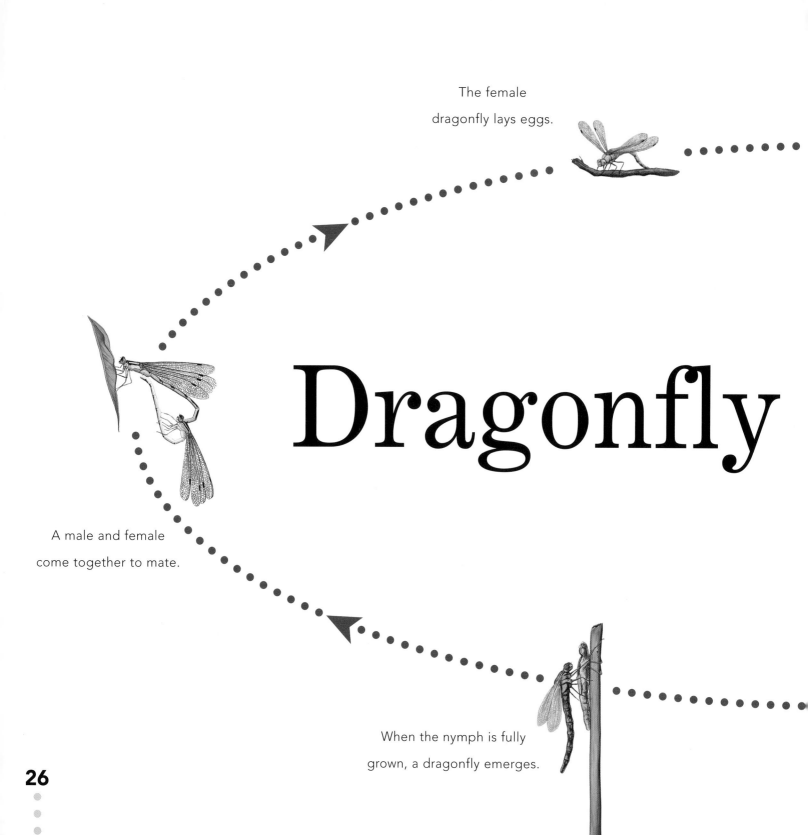

The female
dragonfly lays eggs.

# Dragonfly

A male and female
come together to mate.

When the nymph is fully
grown, a dragonfly emerges.

Some dragonfly eggs
are long and thin.

The eggs hatch
into nymphs
underwater.

# CIRCLE OF LIFE

The nymphs shed their
skin as they grow.

**breeding site** A place where insects mate and females can lay their eggs.

**claspers** A pair of appendages at the end of a male dragonfly's abdomen that it uses to hold a female when they mate.

**climates** Weather conditions usually found in a particular place.

**compound eyes** Eyes made up of thousands of tiny lenses.

**fossils** The preserved remains of prehistoric animals and plants.

**gills** The organ through which a nymph breathes underwater.

**hover** To stay in one place in the air.

**lenses** Transparent structures that focus light in eyes.

**nymphs** The young form of dragonflies after they hatch from eggs.

**pterodactyl** A large flying reptile that existed in prehistoric times.

**segments** The many parts into which something is divided.

**sperm** Fluid produced by male animals that makes a female's eggs grow into babies.

**tadpole** The small, swimming larva of a frog.

**veins** Hollow tubes that form the framework of an insect's wing.

**wing cases** A pair of strong wings that cover a dragonfly's flying wings.

Published by Smart Apple Media

1980 Lookout Drive

North Mankato, Minnesota  56003

Illustration: Desiderio Sanzi

Design: Deb Miner

**Library of Congress**

**Cataloging-in-Publication Data**

Morris, Ting.

Dragonfly / by Ting Morris.

p. cm. — (Creepy crawly world)

Summary: An introduction to the physical
characteristics, behavior, and life cycle of
dragonflies.

ISBN 1-58340-380-9

1. Dragonflies—Juvenile literature.

[1. Dragonflies.] I. Morris, Ting. II.Title.

QL620.M675 2003

595.7'33—dc21   2002044646

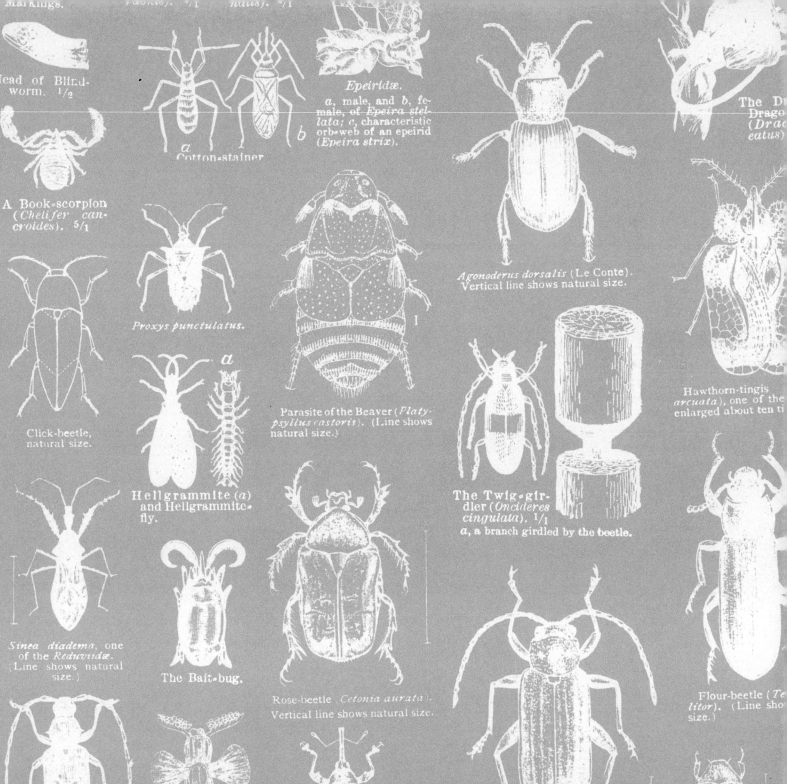

Markings.

Head of Blind-worm. 1/2

A Book-scorpion (*Chelifer cancroides*). 5/1

Cotton-stainer

*Epeiridæ.*
*a*, male, and *b*, female, of *Epeira stellata*; *c*, characteristic orb-web of an epeirid (*Epeira strix*).

The D
Drago
(*Dra
eatus*)

*Agonoderus dorsalis* (Le Conte). Vertical line shows natural size.

*Proxys punctulatus.*

Click-beetle, natural size.

Hellgrammite (*a*) and Hellgrammite-fly.

Parasite of the Beaver (*Platypsyllus castoris*). (Line shows natural size.)

Hawthorn-tingis *arcuata*), one of the enlarged about ten ti

The Twig-girdler (*Oncideres cingulata*). 1/1
*a*, a branch girdled by the beetle.

*Sinea diadema*, one of the *Reduviidæ*. (Line shows natural size.)

The Bait-bug.

Rose-beetle (*Cetonia aurata*). Vertical line shows natural size.

Flour-beetle (*Te litor*). (Line sho size.)

*Galeruca notata*

Ground-beetle (*Caloso
alidum*), natural size.

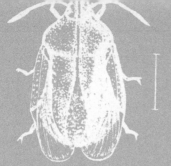

Spiderwort Owlet-moth (*Prodenia flavimedia*).
*a*, larva ; *b*, wings of moth.

Apple
p
s, sipl

*Eurygaster   alternatus ;*
wings partly open. (Line shows
natural size.)

Thighed Metapodius (*Metapo-
dius femoratus*).

The Cucujo.

*Ephemeridæ.*
uropean May-fly (*Eph-
ulgata*) and its sub-
arva.

Bombardier-beetle (*Bra-
chinus stygicornis*). (Vertical line shows natural size.)

*Podisus placidus.*
*a*, enlarged ; *b*, natural size.

H
Tail
ing hor
dal ver
dal ra
bones;
esses o
united
for the
ral spir

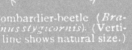

*Libellulidæ.*
Development of a dragon-fly,
showing the subaquatic larva,
mergence from the pupa, and
he adult fully winged insect.

A Flea (*Pulex irri-
tans*).
*a*, puncturing stylets of
the proboscis.

A Bristletail
(*Lepisma sac-
charina*). $^{5}/_{1}$

*Phymata erosa.*

*Atypus sulzeri.* (Vertical line
shows natural size.)

Bacon-
beet'c.

One of

Grape-vine    Fidia
(*F. viticida*). (Line
sh ws natural size.)